HATSHEPSUT

T.D. VAN BASTEN

HISTORY PLAZA

www.historyplaza.com

© 2016 All Rights Reserved

Copyright © 2016 by T.D. van Basten
ISBN: 978-1523478996
Published by History Plaza
First Printing, January 2016

The right of T.D. van Basten to be identified as author of this work has been asserted by him in accordance with sections 77 and 78 of the Copyright, Designs and Patents Act 1988.

All rights reserved. No part of this publication may be reproduced, stored in retrieval system, copied in any form or by any means, electronic, mechanical, photocopying, recording or otherwise transmitted without written permission from the publisher. You must not circulate this book in any format.

Thank you for buying an authorized edition of this book and for complying with copyright laws by not reproducing, scanning, or distributing any part of it in any form without permission. You are supporting writers and allowing History Plaza to continue to publish books for every reader. Thank you for respecting the hard work of this author.

www.historyplaza.com

Table of Contents

Introduction 1

I: Egypt on the Rise 5
The Beginning of the 18th Dynasty 9
Thutmose I 12

II: A Royal Path 17
Daughter of a King 21
Great Royal Wife and God's Wife of Amun 22
From Co-Regent to Pharaoh 27

III: Senenmut and Hatshepsut 33

IV: The Disappearance of Hatshepsut 37
Condemnation to Oblivion 40
Hatshepsut's Tomb 43

V: The Legacy of Hatshepsut 49
Legacy to Egypt 52

Legacy to the World 54

Conclusion 57

A Note from T.D. van Basten 61

About the Author 63

Ancient Egypt Biographies 65

INTRODUCTION

Hatshepsut was arguably the most powerful female to rule as pharaoh during its long and storied history in the wealthy Egypt of the New Kingdom. Her rule was highly unconventional, yet she had the support of the power brokers at the time. Somehow, during her long reign as pharaoh with her stepson, she managed to maintain positive relationships with the right constituency, as well as her co-ruler. It would seem likely that, if there was internal strife within the royal house as to the moves made by Hatshepsut, there would be some documentation or indication of this tension in the historical record. As of the time of this writing, no evidence of poor relations or civil strife has ever been found.

Growing up in a powerful royal family, she was, from birth, a woman of greater power than ordinary. As the only surviving daughter of the pharaoh Thutmose I, it was known early on that her destiny was to be Queen. This means that she had the benefits of education and training that most could not even dream of receiving. Her early participation in religious rituals and rites also helped her develop connections with highly influential people within the cult of Amun that was growing immensely in power and wealth during the New Kingdom.

As it turns out, her destiny had something far greater in store. She did not come to power all at once, nor did she take or keep the throne by force. She married her half-brother and incoming pharaoh, Thutmose II, at a very young age. From all accounts, her husband was very reliant on Hatshepsut's opinion and input. This gave her an unprecedented level of power for a woman.

In addition to being the Great Royal Wife of the pharaoh, and having his ear as well, she was also given the title of God's Wife of Amun. This title gave her even more power. During her era, the priests of Amun were among the most powerful individuals in Egypt behind the pharaoh himself. As God's Wife of Amun, she was the most powerful priestess in all of Egypt, also meaning she was more powerful than even the high priests themselves.

It was due to these relationships that she cultivated as the proverbial ear of the pharaoh and one of the most powerful religious figures in all of Egypt, which gave her the power she needed to make the unprecedented move of taking the throne.

Her half-brother died at a young age, leaving only his young son, Thutmose III, as the heir. The son of one of his lesser wives, Thutmose III took the throne when he was a mere infant. As was tradition, Hatshepsut became his co-regent, essentially serving in his place until he came of age. However, somewhere along the way, for reasons that are lost to history, Hatshepsut took the throne and became pharaoh of Egypt along with Thutmose III, apparently with the support of the power brokers of the time.

As king, she oversaw immense renovations and restorations, as well as the construction of beautiful temples, obelisks, and her famous mortuary temple. The death of this enigmatic woman is shrouded in mystery. She seemingly disappears from history sometime after year 22 of their rule. Her successor, Thutmose III, would, at various times during his rule, undertake a bizarre, haphazard campaign to destroy all likeness of Hatshepsut as king and pharaoh. The lackluster effort of this campaign meant that much was left for posterity.

The 18th Dynasty
The Beginning
1550 B.C. – 1400 B.C.

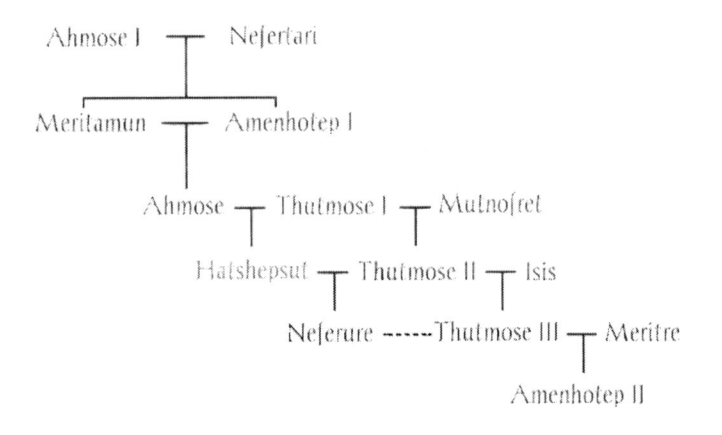

```
Ahmose I ─┬─ Nefertari
          │
   ┌──────┴──────┐
Meritamun ─┬─ Amenhotep I
           │
      Ahmose ─┬─ Thutmose I ─┬─ Mutnofret
              │              │
         Hatshepsut ─┬─ Thutmose II ─┬─ Isis
                    │                │
              Neferure ------ Thutmose III ─┬─ Meritre
                                            │
                                      Amenhotep II
```

I

EGYPT ON THE RISE

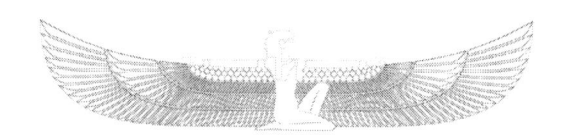

The 18th dynastic period in Egypt is one of the most well-known and documented of all periods in ancient Egyptian history. Many refer to this as the period of "the stars" as this dynasty includes some of the most famous of all of Egypt's many rulers – from Hatshepsut to the Heretic King Akhenaten, his wife Nefertiti and the boy-king Tutankhamen. The start of the 18th dynasty also marks the transition from the Second Intermediate Period to the New Kingdom.

This period is sometimes referred to as the Thutmosid Dynasty, as many see the rule of Thutmose I as the "true beginning" of the New Kingdom. The New Kingdom is the most well documented period in Egyptian history and also marks perhaps its most prosperous times. It was during this period that Egypt's borders, power, and influence were at their peak height.

Thought to have begun sometime around 1550 B.C., Ahmose I was the first ruler of the 18th dynasty, even though many see Thutmose as the "true start" of this dynasty. However, there were two rulers before Thutmose that need to be introduced.

Ahmose I, the first ruler of the 18th dynasty is thought of as the transitional king between the Second Intermediate Period and the New Kingdom. His reign was followed by that of his son, Amenhotep I, which is thought to have been a relatively uneventful period during Egyptian history.

Historians speculate that Amenhotep I did not produce a male heir and that his successor, the famous Thutmose I, was a relation of royal blood, but not a child of Amenhotep. It was imperative that the pharaoh has royal blood, but perhaps more important was that he marries a woman of royal lineage as the divine nature of the pharaoh's rule was transmitted through the female blood line.

Some have used this as reasoning to claim that Egypt was actually a matriarchal society, but there is much more evidence that works against this theory than that supports it. While the royal blood line was passed down through the women, this did not grant them the same kind of power that their husbands were granted as pharaoh. They were often depicted as submissive to their husbands, working stridently to help support his kingship and produce the future heir to the throne.

The beginning of the New Kingdom was one of immense territorial expansion, a reunification of Upper and Lower Egypt, and a dramatic increase in Egypt's regional power and influence. It was during the beginning of this period that the Egyptians were finally able to drive out the dreaded Hyksos, their long-time rival, once and for all. It is easy to see why this is such an interesting time for Egyptian scholars to cover. This was a period of reunification. A period of dramatic expansion. And it was also a period where many revolutionary things occurred, from the longest-ruling female pharaoh, Hatshepsut, to the so-called Heretic King, Akhenaten and the Amarna Heresy.

It should also be noted that the rulers of the New Kingdom were incredibly prolific builders and they left a good deal of documentation about their rule. This has allowed us a better glimpse into the life and times of New Kingdom rulers than we have for any other time period in ancient Egyptian history.

THE EGYPT OF HATSHEPSUT

1

The beginning of the New Kingdom was one of immense territorial expansion, a reunification of Upper and Lower Egypt, and a dramatic increase in Egypt's regional power and influence.

The Beginning of the 18th Dynasty

The "founder" (if you will) of the New Kingdom, Ahmose I, is also seen as the last ruler of the Second Intermediate Period. The exact dates of his reign are debated by historians, but it is thought that he came to power sometime around 1550 B.C. He ascended to the throne as a young boy and is believed to have ruled as king for some 25 years.

He was thought to be around 10 years of age when his father died and he ascended to the throne. Due to his young age, it is likely that his mother, Queen Ashotep, served as co-regent. The evidence from the time shows her as a powerful woman in her own right, giving credence to the idea that she initially ruled the country with her young son.

While there is not a lot known about the early years of his rule, an autobiography by a naval officer serving under Ahmose I gives us a better picture. The officer described various military sieges led by Ahmose between the 10th and 15th years of his rule. It was during these battles that the mysterious Hyksos were finally expelled from Heliopolis and the whole of Egypt. Not much is known about the Hyksos. They are mysterious peoples. What we do know about them is that they were a long-time rival and foe of Egypt.

In addition to expelling the Hyksos and the reunification of Upper and Lower Egypt, Ahmose I is also responsible for a huge increase in territorial expansion. His campaigns stretched the borders of Egypt into Nubia and past the Second Cataract of the Nile. These territorial expansions not only brought greater swaths of territory under Egypt's control, it also gave Egypt power and control over a vast amount of wealth and natural resources that dramatically improved the financial state of the growing empire.

The successor to Ahmose I was his son, Amenhotep I. Amenhotep I ruled from roughly 1526-1506 B.C., and was the third son of King Ahmose I and Queen Ahmose-Nefertari. He was not originally selected to ascend to the throne upon the death of his father. However, though the details are murky, it appears that both of Amenhotep's older brothers died before their father, leaving Amenhotep next in line for the kingship.

There is not a lot of documentation or evidence that survives to tell us much about the reign of Amenhotep I, but many scholars claim that his was a stable, but also uneventful period of rule. It appears that he was able to maintain a unified Egypt and control over the territory captured by his father. There is no indication that he undertook any further efforts at territorial expansion. He is credited with a number of rebuilding and restoration projects in Upper Egypt.

THE BEGINNING OF THE 18TH DYNASTY

2

The reign of Amenhotep I is thought to have been a relatively uneventful period during Egyptian history. He is credited with a number of rebuilding and restoration projects in Upper Egypt.

Thutmose I

Thutmose I ("Thoth bore him") was the third king of the 18th dynasty of the New Kingdom. His parentage is disputed. Some historians believe that he is the son of Amenhotep I and one of his concubines or lesser wives. Others claim that Amenhotep fathered no sons and that Thutmose is simply a royal relation that was deemed a suitable successor to the throne. The true nature of his origins may be permanently lost to history. Despite the mystery, he took the throne and oversaw one of the most prosperous times of Egyptian history.

During his reign, Thutmose I expanded the borders of the Egyptian empire farther than any other time in the history of country. This expansion saw the borders of Egypt extend even further into Nubia, as well as into the Levant. These territorial expansions sent a clear message as to who controlled the region to other civilizations. It also gave Egypt possession of gold and other valuable resources that would drastically improve the wealth of the nation and set the stage for the bounty of the New Kingdom.

Though there is speculation that his predecessor, Amenhotep, may have been buried there, Thutmose I is the first confirmed kingly burial in the famous Valley of the Kings. Thus far, no evidence of the tomb of Amenhotep I—although KV39 is a possible candidate—has been found, so Thutmose I still has the honor of being the first "official" kingly burial in this incredibly famous royal burial complex. There are a total of two tombs located in the Valley of the Kings that are associated with Thutmose I. However, while examining tomb KV38, it is thought that Thutmose was moved from KV20 (which is also associated with Hatshepsut). We know that, throughout history, these tombs were repeatedly plundered and many of the tombs would be filled with silt as a result of flash floods, or simply caved in due to lack of structural integrity.

It is generally thought that he ruled from 1506-1493 B.C. Pinpointing exact dates in ancient history is almost impossible, especially when it comes to the ancient Egyptians. They used a dating system that was based on the length of the rule of the current pharaoh, making it a bit difficult to get truly accurate dates for things. In addition to his famed, highly successful military conquests, Thutmose I was also the overseer of a variety of important building projects. Most famously were his contributions to the highly sacred Temple of Karnak. These projects were undertaken, as was Thutmose's mortuary temple, by the architect, Ineni. These additions marked the greatest expansions of the temple complex in Egypt's long history.

He also initiated the building of statues, stele, and administrative buildings in many places throughout the country including Abydos, Memphis, Edfu, and more. It is through his massive constructions and multitude of inscriptions that we know so much about this storied pharaoh.

Upon his death, Thutmose I was succeeded by his son, Thutmose II, and shortly thereafter, his daughter Hatshepsut would take the throne. His daughter would become the longest-ruling female pharaoh in all of Egypt's storied history and she would be one of the most successful, but revolutionary, leaders the country ever saw. Her rule was very prosperous, but dramatic campaigns to erase all traces of her rule were undertaken in earnest upon her death.

Hatshepsut was the first female to claim the title of king at the same time of another king—her stepson Thutmose III. It was also the only time in Egyptian history where the nation was controlled by two pharaohs ruling the whole region altogether. There is archeological evidence that at least one previous female pharaoh has ever existed during the 12th dynasty, named Queen Sobekneferu. Though, there are more possible candidates to have been pharaoh before Hatshepsut, such as Nitocris of the 6th dynasty, however, they are not confirmed by archeological records. Nevertheless, none of them was pharaoh together with another one and they were no match to the power and success of Pharaoh Hatshepsut.

During the years of Hatshepsut's reign as king, she made most of the political decisions and attended to the ruling of the country. Thutmose III however, was never "de-throned." He always kept his title as king and pharaoh, Hatshepsut merely claimed the same titles for herself as well.

Thutmose I was the overseer of a variety of important building projects. Most famously were his contributions to the highly sacred Temple of Karnak.

THUTMOSE I

II

A ROYAL PATH

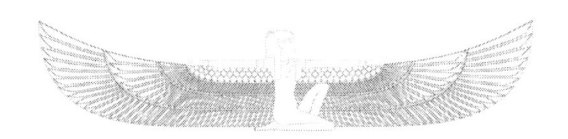

As daughter of one of the most powerful pharaohs in Egyptian history, Hatshepsut was born in an Egypt at the height of its influence and power. Hatshepsut's very name implied her future as it meant "Foremost of the Noble Ladies." Her high born status was evident in her name and her role in the future was quite clear from the start. As the only surviving daughter of Thutmose I and his Great Royal Wife, Hatshepsut would go on to become the longest ruling Egyptian female. There was no way she could know her fate at such a young age.

In addition to her success as a female ruler, she was also a highly successful pharaoh in her own right. She would lead Egypt through one of its most stable and prosperous times. Gender aside, one would be hard pressed to argue that she was an unfit ruler. There is growing evidence that, more than anything, her being a female and thus, her rule going against Ma'at, explain why she was erased from history. While many argue otherwise, there is no real evidence of animosity between stepmother and stepson that would explain his decision to haphazardly try to erase her legacy. She was not just a powerful female, she was powerful in general and this would set the proverbial stage for the enhanced powers and divine status future pharaohs could (and would) claim.

Her first brush with power occurred at a very young age. At the tender age of 12, Hatshepsut was married to her half-brother, Thutmose II, as he had become pharaoh. It appears that he was a rather ineffectual leader and that Hatshepsut held quite a sway over him, indicating that she had a lot of power, even early on. There is a lot of evidence to support the theory that, while he may have verbalized the decisions, they were either decided upon mutually, or perhaps even by Hatshepsut herself.

After the death of her young husband, Hatshepsut managed to retain power by becoming co-regent with Thutmose II's son, Thutmose III. While it was traditional for a royal mother to serve as co-regent with her young son until he came of age, there was no precedent for a stepmother to do the same. The details surrounding the decision for Hatshepsut, and not Thutmose III's birth mother, to serve as co-regent, are murky and highly contentious. Given the importance of the royal bloodline, it is not too far reaching to assume that Hatshepsut, as a royal descendant and Queen, had a much more legitimate right to co-regency than Thutmose's birth mother.

As Thutmose III was just a young child at the time of his father's death, Hatshepsut, as co-regent, would have been in charge of the running of the country. During this time, she continued to cultivate relationships with the very powerful high priests of the cult of Amun. It was during the 18th dynasty that the cult of Amun was ascending to the heights of their power, wealth, and influence, so they were a powerful constituency for Hatshepsut. It was during the New Kingdom that the cult of Amun saw an unprecedented rise in power and prestige. The High Priests of Amun would gain almost as much power and wealth as the pharaoh himself. And due to their positions with the mighty gods, it is likely to they were even more powerful to regular people than the king.

In what has gone down in history as one of the most revolutionary and bold "power grabs," Hatshepsut declared herself pharaoh and King of Egypt sometime during the 7th year of their co-regency. This gave her the same level of power and legitimacy that Thutmose III had. The circumstances that led to this drastic maneuver have been much debated since the 19th century when Hatshepsut was "rediscovered."

There is no indication that she neglected and/or had any ill-intentions towards Thutmose III, as he retained all his royal titles and still appeared (though along with her now) as pharaoh in formal depictions. Due to the unconventional nature of her rule, she expended a lot of effort reinforcing the legitimacy of her kingship. She was very concerned that there was a clear indication of her divine lineage, which is what gave the king his claim to the throne. She would rewrite her own history and be very cognizant in how she portrayed herself as a leader during her long rule.

Whether or not all of these efforts were necessary is not known, but clearly she felt it was important that her rule was imbued with all the divine elements and royal privilege that all male pharaohs enjoyed. She was, in no way, the only ruler in ancient history to alter her back story in order to support the "rightness" of her rule. This was common practice.

As she was a female and so much of the lore of the pharaoh surrounded his general "maleness," it seems she felt the need to show that she could still do all the things that they expected of a male pharaoh and that she had come to power under the same divine leadership as any other pharaoh. This would explain why she is shown with masculine pharaonic garb and sometimes, even depicted as a male.

Daughter of a King

Hatshepsut was the only surviving child of Thutmose I and his Great Royal Wife, Ahmose. As she was the only surviving child (she had a sister who died at a young age), it was well known that her future was as Queen. She would have been groomed for this important future role from a young age. This meant she would receive training and education that would prepare her for her role and give her the skills she needed to perform her ritual functions.

Due to her stature and royal future, she was able to obtain skills and knowledge that was generally reserved for a very select few, predominately males. She would have understood from a young age how to properly act in certain situations, how to interact with different segments of royal and religious society, and more. Around the time she was 12, her father, Thutmose I, died. As she was the only surviving royal child, the throne went to her step-brother, Thutmose II. He was the son of Thutmose I and one of his lesser wives, Mutnofret. Following tradition, Hatshepsut would marry her step-brother and become his chief consort and Great Royal Wife.

Great Royal Wife and God's Wife of Amun

Hatshepsut would have known from a very young age that she would become the future Queen of Egypt. As was mentioned, following tradition in royal families, she would marry her closest male relative upon the death of her father. When Thutmose I died, she married her step-brother, Thutmose II, and became his Great Royal Wife. This title gave her a great deal of power and much indicates that she had a great influence over Thutmose II.

She and Thutmose II were married at a very young age. She was around 12 at the time and it is thought that Thutmose II was even younger. Upon their marriage, Hatshepsut became his Great Royal Wife and also, the most powerful woman in all of Egypt.

It was incredibly important for Thutmose II to take Hatshepsut as his wife, especially since he was only her step-brother. We know that in ancient Egypt, the royal bloodline, and thus the so-called "order of succession," was passed on through the females of the family, not the males. This meant that the incoming pharaoh needed a wife of royal blood as a means to give his rule the divine legitimacy the position required.

In addition to the powerful title of Great Royal Wife, Hatshepsut also bore the title of God's Wife of Amun, making her even more powerful than she would have otherwise been.

During the 18th dynasty, the cult of Amun saw a dramatic increase in power and reach throughout Egypt. Over time, the high priests of Amun would become second only to the pharaoh in terms of power and wealth. There would be a time, later in the 18th dynasty, where the high priests of Amun would attain a position of wealth and power that was actually greater than the pharaoh himself.

As the cult of Amun was an increasingly important part of Egyptian religious and political life, the title of God's Wife of Amun was created for ritual functions. A similar title had been used during certain times in prior to the 18th dynasty, but was associated with a number of different cult gods. It wasn't until the 18th dynasty that the cult of Amun would become the driving force of Egyptian religious life.

The rulers of the 18th dynasty were from Thebes, where the local god was called Amun. It was under these rulers that Egypt was finally able to drive out the dreaded Hyksos, their mysterious rivals, and reunite Upper and Lower Egypt. As Amun was the patron god of these leaders, they thought that it was Amun who had been the driving force behind the successes of their military campaigns.

This does much to explain the seemingly sudden, dramatic increase in the power of this cult.

This powerful title, during the 18th dynasty, was accorded to the mother or Great Royal Wife of the king. A myth developed that Amun actually impregnated the mother of the king, giving him a truly divine parentage. Before this time, kings only became gods or divinities upon their death. Due to this semi-divine parentage, the kings of the 18th dynasty were seen as demigods.

Upon becoming Thutmose II's Great Royal Wife, Hatshepsut also took on the title of God's Wife of Amun. This made her the most powerful priestess in the already powerful cult of Amun. This title garnered her unprecedented amount of power. It also marks the beginning of her rise to power as a kingly ruler in her own right.

Though many elements of the role of the God's Wife of Amun are unknown, we do know that she was seen as the god's primary consort. She was responsible for providing offerings, purification, and would also act as the god's wife during important rituals and festivals.

While performing the ritual functions that being the God's Wife of Amun entailed, Hatshepsut began to cultivate highly important relationships with various members of the cult of Amun. It was this powerful constituency that would later support her ascent to the throne and rule as well.

It appears that, even after the death of her husband, Thutmose II, she retained this title for a while. Thutmose II and Hatshepsut only had one child, a daughter named Neferure. As per tradition, Neferure would go on to marry Thutmose III and would eventually inherit the title of God's Wife of Amun. In fact, Neferure became God's Wife of Amun when Hatshepsut took the role of pharaoh, as it was not possible to be God's Wife of Amun while being pharaoh at the same time.

GREAT ROYAL WIFE AND GOD'S WIFE OF AMUN

<u>4</u>

Hatshepsut was born in an Egypt at the height of its influence and power. Hatshepsut's very name implied her future as it meant "Foremost of the Noble Ladies."

FROM CO-REGENT TO PHARAOH

As the highest "ranking" royal female Hatshepsut would, upon the death of her husband, act as co-regent with her young stepson, Thutmose III. While it was quite common for a king's mother to serve as co-regent with her son until he came of age, Hatshepsut was not Thutmose III's mother, rather, she was his step-mother.

It isn't entirely clear why Hatshepsut, rather than Thutmose III's birth mother, served as co-regent. A common theory is that his mother was a concubine or woman of non-royal blood. It was because of this that Hatshepsut was seen to have more legitimacy as co-ruler than would the birth mother.

Regardless of the exact reasons why, Hatshepsut began to act as co-regent for her young stepson, sometime around 1473 B.C. As co-regent, Hatshepsut would have handled all the details and decisions involved in ruling a powerful country. As was tradition, this was a position she would hold until Thutmose III came of age and was able to take over as sole ruler of the country.

During the beginning of their co-rule, it appears that Hatshepsut had no problem taking the proverbial "backseat" to her stepson. She was always depicted behind him, in a slightly submissive posture that denoted his superiority. However, sometime during the 7th year of their co-rule, she made a bold move and claimed the title of pharaoh and asserted herself a king of Egypt. She took control of the throne and began to rule as the king of the nation, taking the power away from Thutmose III.

Quickly after claiming her title, Hatshepsut took on even more special titles, reserved for the king only, called a "nomen" and "prenomen." These special titles were depicted within a royal cartouche, which is a special circle that encloses the pharaoh's name and indicates his, or her, divine importance. The nomen of Hatshepsut is "Khnumt-Amun Hatshepsut," which means "Joined with Amun, Foremost of Noble Ladies," and her prenomen is Maatkare, meaning "spirit of harmony and truth."

The circumstances surrounding this revolutionary decision are unknown so speculations abound. Some claim that she merely took advantage of her situation and took over. Others speculate that there may have been another royal power grab within the country or some political turmoil that necessitated she took this dramatic move. On the one hand you have those convinced that she made a shrewd decision to gain personal power for herself, on the other, she was doing what she thought needed to be done to safeguard the kingship for her family.

Whatever the reason, she took control over Egypt not as Queen or co-regent, but as pharaoh with the full power that this title entails. This title accorded her with the same power and divine lineage as all other pharaohs in Egyptian history.

Hatshepsut was a smart woman and a shrewd politician. She understood what a dramatic departure from tradition her role implied. It was because of this that she spent so much effort in cultivating the idea of her divine lineage and legitimate claim to the throne. She essentially rewrote her own history to help create the image of a long-understood divine inheritance.

She began to claim that her father, Thutmose I, had not intended for her to become a mere Queen, but that she was actually named as his successor to the throne. She used the common myth of the cult of Amun whereby Amun impregnated her mother, giving her the same semi-divine nature that the other kings of her era possessed.

As a further means of demonstrating her power and the legitimacy of her rule, she was often depicted either as a male, or as a female wearing traditional pharaonic garb such as the fake beard of the king, the double crown which symbolized the Pharaoh's rule over Upper and Lower Egypt, as well as in military headdress.

Despite the tentative nature of her claim to the throne, Hatshepsut was a highly successful ruler. She oversaw a number of building and restoration projects during her lifetime. Her most lasting monument was her mortuary temple located in Deir el-Bahri. This beautiful temple is arguably one of the most exquisite pieces of ancient Egyptian architecture.

We know from reliefs and other wall carvings that she oversaw an incredibly successful expedition to the mysterious land called Punt. Her forces returned from Punt laden with luxury goods from ivory, precious metals, incense, leopard skins, and even dancing girls.

It should be noted that her stepson, who would also become her successor, was not hidden away or mistreated during Hatshepsut's rule. During the 20 years of her rule, Thutmose III received all the traditional training and education that he would need to be a successful future pharaoh. He went on a variety of successful military campaigns during Hatshepsut's reign and made quite the name for himself on the battlefield.

Despite the fact that she was almost erased from history, there is little evidence to indicate that Hatshepsut and Thutmose III had a bad relationship or that he felt any bitterness over the actions she took when it came to assuming the throne.

Hatshepsut is one of a kind and though, as we will soon learn, future leaders tried to erase all evidence of her rule, she could never be fully erased. As more and more was uncovered about this enigmatic woman, the more we learned of her great reach and power. She stands apart from the other females who ruled over Egypt during its storied history in that she is the only one who ever wore the double crown and took on the true role of king and pharaoh with full power for a long time and with such success, including the back-story of divine lineage, even though there were efforts to be erased of the historical records of Egypt.

THE EGYPT OF HATSHEPSUT

III

SENENMUT AND HATSHEPSUT

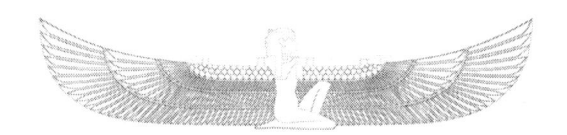

Enigmatically, there is no evidence that Hatshepsut ever remarried or had additional children after the death of her husband and half-brother, Thutmose II. There is much to indicate that she had a very close, long-term relationship with one of her stewards, Senenmut, but the exact nature of this relationship remains open for debate. Some claim that Senenmut was merely an important confidante to Hatshepsut as co-regent and pharaoh, others claim that the two were actually long-term lovers.

Senenmut came from a lowly birth and a relatively unremarkable background. He had no royal or otherwise powerful family connections, yet, he will go down as one of the only non-royal Egyptians that we know much about. During the long reign of Hatshepsut, Senenmut would garner more and more power, becoming incredibly close and influential to the female pharaoh.

We know his parents, Ramose and Hatnufer, were simple peasants, hailing from an area in Egypt called Iuny. That we know of them at all is of significant interest. Outside of the pharaohs and their families, we know more about this administrator and his family than we do about many high priests and other powerful figures in Egyptian history. This is due to the fact that during Senenmut's career, he was able to build his parents an elaborate tomb, which was found, undiscovered, in the 1930s.

This rare, lower class burial gave us a lot of insight into the lives of regular people in Egypt, as well as the obvious power and influence this low born man had on the most powerful figure in Egypt, the pharaoh.

There is much pictorial evidence that Senenmut never married or had children, which some point to as further evidence that he and Hatshepsut were actually lovers, as well as colleagues. In the tomb of the one he built for his parents, he is always depicted alone, or with his parents. This is true even in scenes where it is traditional to portray a man's wife. It is also known that Senenmut's brother performed his funerary rituals, as opposed to a son, which was tradition. This too indicates that Senenmut never married or fathered children.

Exactly how Senenmut and Hatshepsut met is unknown. The first mention of him is as Steward of the God's Wife and Steward of the King's Daughter (Neferure). This indicates that he came to serve the royal family while Hatshepsut was still Queen, married to her half-brother. Or perhaps he arrived shortly after the death of the king while she was acting as co-regent for her young stepson, Thutmose III.

Upon her ascent to the throne, Senenmut was given the title of High Steward of the King. This was an incredibly prestigious and powerful title. Many of his duties during his long career serving Hatshepsut are unknown. We do know that, among the wide variety of responsibilities he held, he was a tutor to Hatshepsut's daughter, Neferure, as well as an overseer of many building projects.

He depicts himself overseeing the completion of obelisks and also takes credit for the oversight and building of Hatshepsut's stunning mortuary temple in Deir el-Bahri, which is located right at the entrance to the famous Valley of the Kings.

We know that he was able to commission the construction of a burial complex for himself. This is something that is pretty much unheard of for someone of lowly birth. His tomb is located near Hatshepsut's and even has what has been called the earliest Egyptian star map on the ceiling of the construction.

Those who support the theory that Senenmut and Hatshepsut were lovers point to much circumstantial evidence to support this idea, including the inclusion of his name and likeness in Hatshepsut's temples and monuments. We are left with many images of Senenmut partaking in activities of power and prestige, as well as with an intimate connection to the kingship.

Perhaps the most famous artwork of Senenmut is the statue that portrays him as the tutor for young Neferure. This statue depicts young Neferure on Senenmut's lap, a very close and intimate position that is only suitable for someone very close to the royal family. The fact that this likeness was even carved indicates the closeness of his relationship with the kingship.

Despite the variety of evidence, the true nature of the relationship between Senenmut and Hatshepsut may never be known. There are some who claim that he was simply a dedicated and loyal follower of the kingship, whereas others note that the evidence indicates that he had a personal, romantic relationship with Hatshepsut. While highly unfounded, this has also led some to speculate that he was actually Neferure's father, though the evidence to support this claim is pretty much non-existent.

IV

THE DISAPPEARANCE OF HATSHEPSUT

Due to the sheer length of time that has passed, as well as the deliberate attempt to erase her rule from the historical record, there is much about Hatshepsut's rule and the woman herself that we do not know. What we do know is that she was a highly intelligent woman with a keen understanding of the varied requirements of a ruler of her stature. In spite of being a woman, something incredibly unconventional, she was a very successful pharaoh.

The fact remained that she was a female and to many, it was not only unconventional, it went against Ma'at, which is the ancient Egyptian concept of order, truth, and the way things are supposed to be. She was also known as Ma'at-ka-re, which means "spirit of harmony and truth" and she was smart enough to know that going against Ma'at would always present a problem and thus spent a good deal of effort to prove the legitimacy of her claim to the throne.

It is not entirely clear why, but Hatshepsut is often depicted with feminine features, but wearing the traditional garb of the pharaoh such as the double crown, the kilt, and the fake beard. In other representations, she is simply depicted as a male, in the traditional stylized manner we are used to seeing in royal Egyptian artwork.

Some argue that she did this as some form of deception, thought there is no indication that she tried to present herself as a man during any official functions. Others believe that by giving her the traditional garb or depicting her in the traditional, stylized way, it would further legitimize her rule as well as her divine lineage, giving her the same power as any other pharaoh.

The circumstances surrounding her death, from the cause of death to when she actually died, have been lost to history, leaving many to speculate, sometimes wildly. The ambiguity of her seeming disappearance from history has led to a lot of conjecture, including speculation that her stepson and successor had murdered her. Claims like this are backed up by the fact that, late in his rule, Thutmose III made a conscious effort to obliterate Hatshepsut's monuments and any references to her as pharaoh or sole ruler of Egypt.

There is a lot of speculation surrounding why Thutmose III made the decision trying to erase Hatshepsut, as a pharaoh, from history. She seemingly disappears somewhere around year 22 of their reign when her stepson took sole rule of the throne and nation upon her disappearance. As noted above, he did eventually try to erase her kingship from recorded history, however this destruction did not start at the beginning of his reign. He started to put efforts in this decision towards the end of his reign with much mystery surrounding it.

Such an enigmatic woman, naturally, has compelled Egyptologists since the discovery of reliefs that referred to a king that was qualified with feminine pronouns. In the early 1900s, before his famous discovery of the tomb of King Tut, Howard Carter discovered what is humbly designated as KV60. This is a tomb that appears to have been intended for a nurse for the royal family.

The tomb was intentionally destroyed, but mummies were recovered from the tomb. When the tomb was reopened in the early 2000s, a whirlwind of press surrounded claims from the Egyptology community that one of the mummies was none other than the female pharaoh, Hatshepsut. These assertions have yet to be fully substantiated and have led to much controversy and conjecture.

Condemnation to Oblivion

As noted previously, the details surrounding the decision to destroy much of Hatshepsut's legacy remain unclear. Sometime between years 20 and 22 of his rule, Thutmose III ordered the destruction of many monuments, temples, and inscriptions that refer to Hatshepsut as pharaoh. Since there is no record of why this decision was made, or even definitive proof that it was, in fact, Thutmose himself who made the decision, people speculate a variety of different possibilities.

Some of the theories are fairly sound, others don't seem to have much basis in the facts we do have at the current time. The facts we know about the attempted erasure are that the destruction was undertaken in a haphazard manner. The defacers seemed to focus mainly on public structures and inscriptions, leaving much evidence of her existence in private temples and a few burial chambers.

One theory is that Thutmose III, who had been relieved of a good deal of his power for a time by Hatshepsut, harbored deep seated anger and bitterness. Proponents speculate that he had wanted to erase her legacy as soon as he took the throne, but that he had to wait for the still-living supporters of Hatshepsut (some very powerful individuals) to pass on. However, the biggest thing taking away from this theory is that there is no evidence to support the idea that the two ever had a negative or tense relationship. There is nothing to indicate any bitterness on his end. Furthermore, as a commander of armed forces, it seems that he could have easily overrun Hatshepsut and claimed the throne had he really wanted to.

Others claim that the attempted destruction was overseen by Thutmose III as a means of solidifying his own rule as pharaoh. His link to the kingship could have been seen as weak, as he was the child of a king and a non-royal wife.

On the other hand, there are some theories which indicate, according to the archeological records, that most of the changes and modifications made by Thutmose III to the constructions and monuments of Hatshepsut were in order to reuse them as was commonly done by Egyptian rulers.

Towards the end of the reign of Thutmose III, his son, Amenhotep II, became his co-regent and successor. Some argue that, taking advantage of a powerful man at the end of his life, Amenhotep convinced his father to erase the legacy of Hatshepsut and solidify the legitimacy of their family as a royal bloodline.

Still, others posit that she was erased for fear that other women in the future might get ideas of power and try to assert their right to the throne. There is circumstantial evidence that supports this theory, such as the fact that after Hatshepsut, powerful titles for Queens (including the God's Wife of Amun) were used very sporadically before being dropped from use completely. In fact, many of the Great Royal Wives of later pharaohs went completely unnamed.

Finally, some say that Thutmose III attempted to erase Hatshepsut's rule so that future generations did not see him as a co-conspirator for going against Ma'at. Those who support this idea claim that his unorthodox co-regency could take the legitimacy of his rule away.

While there is merit to some of these theories, they are all just speculations, as we simply do not know why or even who made this momentous decision, as there is also evidence that many of the modifications were done in the Amarna period during the revolution of Akhenaten, in order to erase the footprints of the cult to Amun.

Hatshepsut's Tomb

During her reign as Queen, Hatshepsut had begun building a burial tomb and mortuary temple for herself. However, upon her ascent to the throne, it was determined that something more suitable to a semi-divine ruler would be more appropriate. There is evidence to support the idea that she started at least three different burial chambers for herself during her life.

The tomb that we now designate as KV20 was originally intended for her father, Thutmose I. After her ascent to the throne, she had the tomb expanded. It appears that she intended the burial chamber to be the final resting place of her and her father. However, history shows us that this did not happen, though exactly why is not clear. What we do know is that Thutmose III, shortly after he took the throne, commissioned the building of KV38. Here, new grave goods were provided and it is alleged that Thutmose I's remains were re-interred here.

Some speculate that, at this time, Hatshepsut was also moved, perhaps to the tomb of a royal nurse. This tomb, designated as KV60, was found in 1903 by Howard Carter. What he found was a tomb that had been intentionally demolished and ransacked, with two female mummies still present. There has been widely ranging speculation over the years as to who the mummies actually are. Most recently, the idea that one of these mummies might be none other than Hatshepsut have gained proverbial steam.

Even former antiquities minister, Zahi Hawass, supports the idea that one of these female mummies is the remains of the female pharaoh. In 2007, the tomb was reopened, the remains of the mummies were scientifically studied for the first time since their discovery. A team of researchers set about learning whatever they could from the remains themselves, as well as any supporting evidence by way of inscriptions or grave goods. They hoped to be able to piece together the different clues to determine who this mummy actually belonged to.

If this mummy is, in fact, Hatshepsut, the condition of her remains actually tells us much about her physical health at the time of death and perhaps, even, indications as to what caused her ultimate demise. Studies of the remains show that the alleged Hatshepsut was an overweight, middle aged female from roughly the same time period as the female pharaoh.

The body shows indications of arthritis and that the woman had bad teeth that likely caused her much pain. The bones of the mummy are riddled with bone cancer, leading many to believe that this was the cause of her death. Researchers even found the likely culprit. It appears that this woman, when alive, suffered from some sort of skin condition. The cream or salve that was regularly applied to the body as a means of dealing with whatever ailment this was has been found to be carcinogenic, likely leading to the development of the cancer.

During the study of the remains, Hawass went so far as to claim that they had found definitive proof that the mummy was Hatshepsut by way of dental evidence. The mummy in KV60 was missing a particular molar and there was even still tooth root remaining. In a canopic jar, bearing Hatshepsut's kingly name and royal cartouche, was found a molar that matches the missing molar on the mummy. To researchers, this was a strong indication that this mummy was, in fact, the female king herself.

While this may seem quite compelling, more research needs to be done to definitively state whether or not the tooth belongs to the mummy in question. Further muddying the proverbial waters is the fact that much of the data collected during this research was never published publicly. DNA and further analysis will be required for much of the Egyptology community to be convinced that these remains belong to the most powerful woman who ever ruled Egypt.

The problem with over-sensationalized stories like this, much about history becomes a "closed book." What this means is that, with a little marginally supported evidence, certain claims, without any counterarguments, become facts in the minds of average people. Many people remember when the claims of Hawass and Connelly came out that they had definitively found Hatshepsut, but not many people know about the lack of data to support this, the lack of cooperation from the Egyptian antiquities community, as well as the evidence that actually throws doubt upon claims such as this. The true heritage of the mummy found is still not definitively proven and while it is exciting and attractive to consider the "case closed," we might be doing history a disservice by doing so.

HATSHEPSUT'S TOMB

5.

Hatshepsut's stunning mortuary temple in Deir el-Bahri, which is located right at the entrance to the famous Valley of the Kings. This tomb, designated as KV60, was found in 1903 by Howard Carter.

THE EGYPT OF HATSHEPSUT

V

THE LEGACY OF HATSHEPSUT

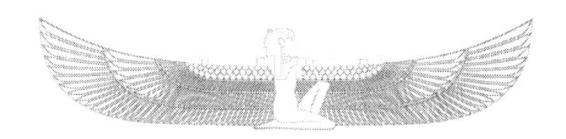

There is a good deal about this powerful woman that we may simply never know. Due to the deliberate efforts to erase her from history, we didn't even begin to learn about her as a ruler in her own right until hieroglyphics were deciphered in the late 1800s. At first, these inscriptions simply raised more questions than they answered. There were a lot of blanks in our knowledge of the time period and many inconsistencies in the things we were uncovering.

We know that her reign was one of economic improvement as well as a time of political stability. She managed to cultivate relationships with a variety of powerful people that were crucial in securing and maintaining approval for her rule. With the help of her advisors, especially Senenmut, she was able to undertake expeditions to faraway lands and return from these successful missions with many riches to show for it.

As we have learned, due to the attempts to erase her from history, not much was known about this incredibly powerful woman until hieroglyphics were deciphered. It was then that researchers noticed the gender inconsistency and feminine portrayals of Hatshepsut with kingly attributes. Deciphering hieroglyphics allowed us the glimpse back into history that we have today. What little we know about the most powerful woman in Egyptian history is thanks to our understanding of their language.

She left an incredible legacy behind her, despite the attempts to strike her rule from the historical record. In Egypt's long and storied history, she was the longest-ruling female to have ever existed. She was also the only female to ever rule as pharaoh with the full powers of such position and with great success in her role, because although there were female pharaohs before and after her, none of them reached the level of leadership and accomplishments of Hatshepsut. Her rule proved that a female was more than capable of handling the tasks that such a position of power would require.

She oversaw an Egypt at the height of its power and prestige. She managed to garner favor from the powerful religious elites that would help support and sustain her rule. She was far from a meek and unassuming ruler. In fact, her rule was more successful than many other male pharaohs we know about. She maintained the vast territorial expansion that occurred under the rule of her father. She made major expeditions to rich, distant lands as a means of procuring additional wealth and resources for the nation. She maintained power and command over all the nomes and outlying regions of territory. There is no indication that hers was a time of economic, political, or civil unrest of any kind.

LEGACY TO EGYPT

Hatshepsut's rule gives Egypt the ability to be claiming to be one of the few nations that have allowed a female to prove her worth as a ruler and leader. She was pharaoh of one of the most powerful countries in the ancient world at the height of Egypt's wealth and power. She was the opposite of an ineffectual leader. She helped solidify Egypt's position of power and wealth within the region, she oversaw dramatically beautiful construction projects, she sent expeditions to faraway lands and returned with riches, and she even oversaw military battles.

In addition to her role in the history of female rulers, she also left behind some of the most beautiful architecture of the New Kingdom. Besides her stunning mortuary temple at Deir el-Bahri, she is also responsible for the erection of at least two obelisks, as well as a number of temples. She also undertook the restoration of a number of Egypt's most holy sites, preserving them for future generations to enjoy. These projects are, in large part, why we have a lot of the relics remaining that we do. Had it not been for the efforts of generations of different royal leaders, so much of the mysterious history of the lands of Upper and Lower Egypt would still remain a mystery.

Her exploits to places like the mysterious land of Punt brought wealth and exotic cultural influence to the country. She was able to maintain positive internal and international relations. Her rule was one of social order and stability. She was, however, by no means weak. Much evidence supports that she was also a warrior too, embracing the warlike an element of the kingship. The expeditions to faraway lands and her willingness to participate in military action as was traditional of the pharaoh, was likely a further key to her success and support as a ruler. She showed the powers that be, through actions, not words, that she "had what it takes" to rule as any man could.

Her father's rule saw the dramatic expansion of Egypt's borders and during her rule, Hatshepsut was able to maintain every inch of this expanded territory. She must also have been highly influential to her stepson and successor, Thutmose III. He would go on to rule as pharaoh upon her death and history knows him as one of the most successful of all of Egypt's many pharaohs. Her legacy is much more far-reaching than just her time as Queen, God's Wife of Amun, co-regent, and pharaoh. She influenced generations of rulers to come and has left a feminist legacy for history that has not been surpassed by any other ancient female ruler in Egypt's long history.

LEGACY TO THE WORLD

One can easily argue that her rule was a powerful move for feminism. What she showed is that, not only can a female handle the stresses of running a powerful nation, she can excel at it too. Hatshepsut showed the ancient world that females were more than competent and capable of handling the rigors of high office. She showed that a female could be a shrewd politician and successful leader and that a woman could gain the respect of her peers and subjects. Whether this was done as a personal power play or as a means to help solidify the future rule of her family line is lost to history. What we do know is that she was king and there is no indication that anyone opposed her rule.

Her rule was one that saw a growth in appreciation for some of the female gods of the Egyptian pantheon like Hathor, Ma'at, and Isis. It appears from some of her actions that she was a supporter of the advancement of the power of women beyond just herself. Indications are that she was very concerned with the grooming and education of her daughter Neferure. Her daughter became the God's Wife of Amun after Hatshepsut, again, giving Neferure a level of power that even a Queen did not generally enjoy. Some argue that Hatshepsut was grooming Neferure to take over her role as pharaoh, but the evidence is shaky and speculative.

Hatshepsut proved that a female could also be a fierce warrior. For many years, she was labeled as a pacifist that never undertook any sort of military campaigns, but there is a lot of evidence that does not support this idea. There is enough evidence via carved reliefs and inscriptions that Hatshepsut ordered at least four different military campaigns during her rule. Whether or not she was an active participant in these battles has been lost to history.

The unconventional nature of her rule is something that always plagued her, leading her to regularly use art and architecture as a means at strengthening her ties to the gods and thus her legitimacy to the throne. One thing is quite clear and that is that she garnered much power and support from highly influential people of the time. It appears that she had full support of the proverbial powers that be for her mysterious ascent to the throne. There are also no indications of any challenges to her kingship in the entirety of her rule.

Given her level of power and influence, it is not a wonder that she is seen as a powerful historical feminist. What is also clear is that her elevation to power struck a chord with the traditional power structure that scared the patriarchy and changed the status of future royal women for many generations to come. She was able to shake that ingrained male power structure and this was something that was seen as increasingly dangerous. Future pharaohs would do much to minimize the role and amount of power Queens had, seemingly as a means of ensuring that there would be no "future Hatshepsut."

As a woman, her whole life is a story of just how successful a woman can be if she is given the opportunity and skills to lead. Even before she became pharaoh, she was a woman of unsurpassed power. She was highly influential to her half-brother and husband, Thutmose II. This has led some to speculate that much of the policy of his kingship was influenced by her. She was given the powerful title of God's Wife of Amun, further strengthening her power and influence. She then went on to serve as co-regent with her stepson until she ascended the throne as pharaoh.

Conclusion

Hatshepsut's name will go down in history for a number of reasons. She was the first and only woman in the storied history of ancient Egypt to rule the country as king and pharaoh while sharing the role with another pharaoh, and having great achievements in her role, elevating the prestige of women as leaders. While there were powerful female rulers and pharaohs before and after her (such as Sobekneferu, Nefertiti and Cleopatra), they did not claim to rule as king. She was also the longest-ruling female leader in the history of Egypt. For these reasons, she is a favorite of many feminist-oriented history buffs. For good reason too, she was not only the first woman to lead as king with full powers and freedom of action, she was well accepted and highly successful as well. She did a lot to further the status of cult goddesses like Hathor, Ma'at, and Isis, as well as trying to engender her daughter with power as well.

She was groomed from the start to be a powerful woman. As the only surviving daughter of a ruling pharaoh, it was known early on that she would become the future Queen of Egypt. This means that she was educated and trained in the skills she would need to perform this role from a young age. Her father died when she was a mere 12 years old. As there were no male heirs from his

Great Royal Wife, it was Thutmose I's son from a lesser wife, Thutmose II, who would claim the throne.

As per custom, Hatshepsut married her half-brother and became the Queen. In addition to this powerful role, she would also be titled God's Wife of Amun. This title made her one of the most powerful religious figures in all of Egypt, serving in ceremony and tradition as the god Amun's wife and chief consort. This powerful, important position also allowed Hatshepsut to cultivate relationships with some of the most important and powerful people in all of Egyptian society.

Her half-brother and husband died at a young age. Thutmose II and Hatshepsut only had a daughter, not a male heir. Like Thutmose II himself, it was the son of a lesser wife that was to be heir to the throne. This son was Thutmose III and he was only an infant when his father died and he was crowned king. As was custom at the time, Hatshepsut stepped in to serve as co-regent until the young pharaoh came of age. This was common practice at the time and though she was his stepmother, not his biological mother, her history and royal lineage made her better suited for co-regency than Thutmose's birth mother.

The details surrounding the event are unknown, but at some point in their co-regency, Hatshepsut ascended the throne as pharaoh and king of Egypt, effectively at the same level of

CONCLUSION

Thutmose III. There is no indication that this situation had any negative impact on the relationship between the two. Hatshepsut's ascension to the throne was supported by the powerful priests of Amun, giving her the backing she needed to maintain her power.

Much surrounding her life and death has been lost to the annals of history and intentional destruction. Though we do not know why, numerous times in the co-ruler reign—Thutmose III, and later in the Amarna period—a campaign to erase her from history was undertaken. Luckily some inscriptions and monuments were able to survive the destruction, giving us the little glimpse into this unconventional history we are left with today.

THE EGYPT OF HATSHEPSUT

A Note from T.D. van Basten

Thank you very much for reading The Egypt of Hatshepsut, If you enjoyed it and found what you were looking for, please be so kind to take a moment to leave a review at your favourite retailer such as Amazon.

I also welcome contact from readers. You can find me on historyplaza.com, and I would be more than happy to get in touch with you. If you enjoy my books, you can also choose to follow me on social media and Amazon to be notified of new releases.

—T.D. van Basten

HISTORY PLAZA
www.historyplaza.com

THE EGYPT OF HATSHEPSUT

About the Author

Born in, what was once known as the Dutch Empire, Timon van Basten found himself in a rather odd time period. Raised and overwhelmed by modern technology during late 20th and early 21st century, he was finally able to overcome the many obstacles through sheer force of character to find his destiny and true passion in life. This passion that we speak of is to provide true value and excessive knowledge to the world. Timon has set the tone for historical coverage and is admired today by many for his exceptional passion, vivid descriptions and storytelling.

Losing sense of time through television and technology, many seem to have forgotten about our ancestors and how the world has been shaped to what it is today. It is here, on History Plaza, where we'll not only focus to make our surroundings aware of our history again, but you'll also find all of the published work of Timon van Basten. Next to his love for reading and writing about history, he also likes to stay in touch with his own readers and visitors. To contact him directly, visit historyplaza.com. You'll also find his monthly articles in the blog section. To get notified of new posts, simply subscribe to the newsletter!

Speaking about blogs... go and see what he's up to! And of course, don't forget to share your thoughts in the comment section with the rest while you're visiting. We love to hear from you!

ANCIENT EGYPT BIOGRAPHIES

THE EGYPT OF CLEOPATRA

Cleopatra VII (69 BC - 30 BC), the last Pharaoh of Egypt, was a very educated, crafty, ambitious and clever woman. Her intellect and charisma—far greater than her beauty and sexuality—allowed her to keep the power for nearly twenty years by fighting against—and allying with—the greatest power at the time, Rome. Although her history was written by who defeated her and, therefore, modified according conveniences of them, there have been found, in recent archaeology researches, evidences of her intellect and achievements that portrayed her beyond her beauty and sexual power. She captivated the two greatest Romans of her time, and destroyed herself. Cleopatra was representing everything that the Romans didn't like. Not only was she a woman, but she was a woman with power.

The Egypt of Nefertiti

For centuries, the beautiful, mysterious Queen Nefertiti, has captured our imaginations. We do not know very much about the woman's origins, or her demise, which only adds to her mysterious appeal. What we do know, however, is that she was the wife of one of the most controversial and radical of all of ancient Egypt's Pharaohs.

Her husband, Akhenaten, often referred to as the "Heretic King" started a revolution for the proto-monotheistic cult of Aten, the sun disk. This revolution led to dramatic social and political changes during what was later called the Amarna Period. From a huge upheaval in the traditional power structure of the nation, the outlaw of traditional gods, and even the relocation of the capital of the nation, there were actually deliberate attempts from the rulers who came after to erase this period of Egyptian history from the historical record. And they nearly succeeded.

The Egypt of King Tut

Upon the opening of the famous tomb of King Tutankhamen, Carter and his team found a huge array of sumptuous grave goods. However, they also found a very small tomb, lacking the well-known royal depictions and wide array of different paintings and inscriptions. Even the grave goods, while luxurious, did not seem fit for a king for his journey to the afterlife.

The many mysteries surrounding Tut led to many fantastic rumors, including that of a curse on the tomb of the boy-king. Circumstances and seemingly sudden deaths, fueled by media coverage, helped ignite the rumor that there was a curse on the tomb and that those who worked within it or benefited from the goods within it would suffer a grisly fate. There were just enough bizarre coincidences to fuel the rumors and convince many of the existence of a curse on the tomb of King Tut.

THE EGYPT OF THUTMOSE III

Thutmose III was one of the most known and respected of all of Egypt's pharaohs, regardless of dynasty or time period. He ruled during the New Kingdom, which is often seen as the "star-studded" dynasty in ancient Egyptian history because that's the dynasty where many of the "big names" come from. He had the benefit of a lengthy co-rule that allowed him to develop and hone his military skills which would serve him incredibly well during his time in power.

His early life and rule were rather unusual, and he was a powerful person, even when he was just a mere infant. He was the son of Thutmose II and one of his lesser wives of common heritage. Thutmose II was married to the incredibly powerful Queen Hatshepsut, but the two were unable to produce a male heir which meant they had to look to Thutmose II's harem for a suitable successor. Thutmose III was the chosen successor.

THE EGYPT OF RAMSES II

In all of Egypt's long and storied history, Ramses the Great stands out as one of the best known and successful of all. Ruling the country for some 67 years, Ramses II ruled over Egypt during a time of stability and prosperity. His rule was marked by economic prosperity, successful military campaigns, and impressive building projects. He wanted from the very beginnings of his long reign, to ensure that his legacy was sealed, literally in stone, and that reminders of his rule were so ubiquitous that he would not be forgotten. In this, like many other elements of his kingship, he was highly successful and he has gone down in history as a legendary ruler.